Our Animal World

Animal Homes

by Karen Latchana Kenney

amicus readers 1

Say hello to amicus readers.

You'll find our helpful dog, Amicus, chasing a ball—to let you know the reading level of a book.

(A)

1

(2)

Learn to Read

Frequent repetition of sentence structures, high frequency words, and familiar topics provide ample support for brand new readers. Approximately 100 words.

Read Independently

Repetition is mixed with varied sentence structures and 6 to 8 content words per book are introduced with photo label and picture glossary supports. Approximately 150 words.

Read to Know More

These books feature a higher text load with additional nonfiction features such as more photos, time lines, and text divided into sections. Approximately 250 words.

Amicus Readers are published by Amicus
P.O. Box 1329, Mankato, Minnesota 56002

Series Editor   Rebecca Glaser
Book Editor   Wendy Dieker
Series Designer   Kia Adams
Book Designer   Heather Dreisbach
Photo Researcher   Heather Dreisbach

Printed in the United States of America at Corporate Graphics, in North Mankato, Minnesota.

1022
3-2011

10 9 8 7 6 5 4 3 2 1

Library of Congress Cataloging-in-Publication Data
Kenney, Karen Latchana.
  Animal homes / by Karen Latchana Kenney.
     p. cm. – (Amicus readers. Our animal world)
  Includes index.
  Summary: "Describes how different animal homes are used and how they benefit each animal. Examples include nests, caves, webs, tree hollows, termite mounds, and shells. Includes comprehension activity"–Provided by publisher.
  ISBN 978-1-60753-141-8 (library binding)
  1. Animals–Habitations–Juvenile literature. I. Title.
QL756.K47 2011
591.56'4-dc22
                                        2010031470

Table of Contents

Animals make their homes in many places.

nest

4

High in a tree sits a
huge eagle's nest.
There, eagles keep
their chicks safe.

tree
hollow

An opossum lives inside a tree hollow. It lines it with leaves and grass. Inside, it stays safe and dry.

cave

A dark cave is a home for bats. Hanging from the roof, they sleep all day.

mound

African termites build tall mounds from dirt. Warm air escapes from holes at the top. The termites stay cool in rooms below.

termites

hive

12

Honeybees build a hive for their home. Its wax cells store honey. The bees have food all winter long.

web

A spider's home is also
a trap for its food. It spins
a sticky web and waits.
Soon bugs are caught
in its web.

shell

Hermit crabs borrow another animal's old shell for their homes. As they grow, the crabs find bigger shells to live in.

An animal's home is the best place for it to live. How is your home right for you?

Picture Glossary

cave
a large hole
underground or in the
side of a hill or cliff

hive
a nest that bees build
where they live and
make honey

mound
a tell termite nest
made from dirt

20

shell
a hard outer covering that keeps animals safe

tree hollow
a hole in a tree trunk

web
a net of sticky threads that is made by a spider to catch insects

What Do You Remember?

Look at each animal pair and answer the question.

Which makes mounds?

Which lives in a cave?

Which lives in a hive?

If you don't remember, read through the book again for the answers.

Ideas for Parents and Teachers

Our Animal World, an Amicus Readers Level 1 series, gives children fascinating facts about animals with ample reading support. In each book, photo labels and a picture glossary reinforce new vocabulary. The activity page reinforces comprehension and critical thinking. Use the ideas below to help children get even more out of their reading experience.

Before Reading

- Ask: *Can you think of different kinds of animal homes?*
- Discuss any questions students have about animal homes.
- Tell students to read the questions on page 22 so they will recognize the answers as they read the book.

During Reading

- Have students write the photo label words on a piece of paper as they read. Then ask them to guess the meaning of each word.
- Take a picture walk through the book. Ask students to describe what they see.
- After each spread, ask students to retell the content in their own words.

After Reading

- Ask students to look at the glossary. Have them check their guesses with the actual meanings of the words.
- Discuss how each home fits its animal. Ask: *How does this home help the animal live?*
- Ask students to think about their homes. Discuss ways that homes keep people safe and help them live.

23

Index

Web Sites

DragonflyTV: Living Things
http://pbskids.org/dragonflytv/show/livingthings.html

Kidport Reference Library: Animal Homes. http://www.kidport.com/RefLib/Science/AnimalHomes/AnimalHomes.htm

National Geographic Kids: Animals: Creature Features
http://kids.nationalgeographic.com/kids/animals/creaturefeature/

Project Dragonfly. Houses.
http://www.units.muohio.edu/dragonfly/houses/

Photo Credits
Alan Gleichman/Shutterstock, 6–7, 21, 22; Daniel Cox/Oxford Scientific/Getty Images, 18; David Parsons/iStockphoto, 9, 22; First Light/Alamy, 4–5; Florin Tirlea, 22; Giorgio Perbellini/iStockphoto, 14, 22; Joyce Wijnstra/iStockphoto, 10, 20; Michele Westmorland/Getty Images, 1; Oxford Scientific/Getty Images, 16–17, 21, 22; Pete Oxford/Minden Pictures/National Geographic Stock, 12, 20; Piotr Naskrecki/Getty Images, 11, 22; Premierlight Images/Alamy, cover; Sergey Kolesnikov/Dreamstime.com, 8, 20; Tatonka/Dreamstime.com, 21

For Every
Individual...

The
INDIANAPOLIS PUBLIC
Library

**Renew by Phone
269-5222**

**Renew on the Web
www.imcpl.org**

For General Library Infomation
please call 275-4100